THE MANDATE OF PAUL

TOKUNBO EMMANUEL

The Mandate of Paul

Published by
SOPHOS Books Ltd.
2 Woodberry Grove
London
N12 0DR
www.publishwithsophos.com

All Scripture quotations are taken from the *New King James* version of the Bible. Used by permission.
Scriptures marked KJV are from the *King James Version* of the Bible. Used by permission.
Scriptures marked AMP are from the *Amplified Version* of the Bible. Used by permission.

ISBN 978-1-905669-21-9

Cover design by *Maestro Creativity*
Printed in the United Kingdom

CONTENTS

To my family in purpose:
Linda, the wife of my youth;
Destiny, Daniel and David, our angels.

AUTHOR'S PREFACE

The title I originally gave to this book, *The Macedonian Call,* came to me after the Lord had "called" me to return to Nigeria and start my publishing work for Him there. *The Mandate of Paul,* however, fits nicely into the *Bible Characters Inspirational Series* that we are developing at *Sophos Books*. There is so much to learn from Paul's life and I foresee another volume that will go into more depth on some issues.

I have taken the liberty to share bits from my experience at the end of each chapter, but in no way am I putting myself on the same pedestal with Paul the apostle. Readers can also document their own application in the *"Your Story"* sections, thus increasing learning. At some point, I kept to the name Paul even when the context referred to his previous name, Saul. Also, there are some helpful repetition. Please be aware!

I am grateful to a long list of people who continue to make my journey into purpose meaningful. How I would love to list everyone like Paul did in Romans 16! I can only, for space constraints, give thanks to God, my inspiration and Lord. To you be the glory forever!

FOREWORD

Thank God for the gift salvation! There will never be a greater demonstration of God's love than the coming of Jesus Christ to the earth for the ultimate price of our redemption. However, since salvation is not an end in itself, but a means to one, it becomes important for us to know that tied to our *salvation,* is a *purpose* for which we have been created. Tokunbo Emmanuel's new book clearly shows that we will come into this purpose *only* when we fully submit ourselves to Christ's lordship over our lives.

We should not be content with just being saved, but should also let Christ be the Lord who points out the direction we should go. As Lord, He gives us assignments that are intricately linked to our destinies in life. Apostle Paul told Timothy that God has *saved us* and *called us* with a holy calling (2 Timothy 1:6). To know and live out the details of our divine calling remains a nut that must be cracked, as salvation alone can become dull after a period of time if our purpose in life remains unknown or elusive.

Pastor Tokunbo wants us to be thankful to God for our salvation, but also appeals passionately for all to enquire from the Lord about the purpose of their calling. At his conversion, Paul made this enquiry and the Lord revealed it to him. Pastor Tokunbo himself, after his conversion, would have pursued his own plans, but the Lord intercepted him and revealed heavens divine purpose to him - the course that he is still following to date.

The Mandate of Paul, I believe, will encourage readers to dump their personal ambitions and seek the exciting life that heaven has in store for them. The book is full of revelation and godly wisdom. May the Lord use it extensively!

- Bishop Abraham Olaleye

Abraham Evangelistic Ministries (Nigeria)

CHAPTER 1

OUR LORD AND SAVIOUR

(Acts 9:1-6; 2:36)

When Saul encountered Jesus Christ on the road to Damascus, he discovered two important spiritual realities that later became fundamental in his subsequent walk with God. Firstly, he found out that the man Jesus was much more than a religious fanatic who blasphemously declared Himself the awaited Messiah of the Jews. Anyone who had the power to stop him in his tracks and knock him to the ground was certainly not on his level. Such a person should be referred to as "lord."

"Who are you, Lord?" was Saul's answer when he was asked a reason for his religious zeal.

Secondly, the answer that Saul received – *"I am Jesus, whom you are persecuting"* – implied that this Jesus was not just *a lord* but *The Lord* of the Jews, and if He be *The Lord,* then He had authority over his life. After all, his zeal was for the God of his fathers and his conviction was that he was doing his Lord's bidding. Realising the error of his misdirected passion, he asked with fear and astonishment, *"Lord, what do You want me to do?"*

These two aftermaths of Saul's Damascus Road experience are worth considering. We know from Scripture that this encounter was the beginning of Saul's salvation. However, Saul, who later became Paul, did not just receive Jesus into his life as *Saviour*; he also submitted to Jesus as *Lord*. This is the true extent of Christian conversion.

TWO-SIDED CONVERSION

Knowing Jesus Christ as the One who *saves* from sin and death is not enough for a life of purpose on earth. It is only one side of the divine exchange. We *also* need to know Him as *Lord*.

All that Jesus is as Saviour speaks of what He has done *for* us. All that He is as Lord speaks of what He expects *from* us and His authority *over* us. We cannot be true followers of Christ without accepting *both* His salvation and His lordship.

Jesus will freely give rest to those who come to Him with their yokes and heavy burdens; but He *also* expect them to take His yoke upon themselves and learn of Him (Matthew 11:28-30). The former is akin to *salvation* while the latter is a description of Christ's *lordship*. Embracing both makes us disciples of Jesus. Those who want the *salvation* of Jesus but are not ready to follow the *lordship* of Jesus, at best, remain babes in the faith. It is only a matter of time before they become grounded in carnality. The sure antidote to worldliness and spiritual immaturity is following the lordship of Christ – whatever He says and wherever He leads.

> *We cannot be true followers of Christ without accepting both His salvation and His lordship.*

We can conclude in this light, that Paul started his journey of faith aright. It did not take a few years of knowing the salvation of Christ for him to submit to the lordship of Christ. He received Jesus *fully* from day one – as Saviour *and* as Lord – and his life turned around completely.

Those who receive Christ "halfway" do not commit to Him all the way. Their Christian experience is characterised by a constant expectation of receiving something *from* God; very seldom a readiness of giving anything of worth *to* Him. God does not want earthly or material things from us; He wants our life – *all* of our life – and only true disciples give Him everything they have and are. This is fundamental to our walk with God and the determinant of our response to the purpose to which He has called us.

Those who receive Christ "halfway" do not commit to Him all the way.

THIS MAN JESUS

The Greek word translated "salvation" is *soteria*. It always connotes the idea of deliverance, safety, preservation, health and prosperity. All these belong to us because of Jesus, the One anointed of God to be our Saviour. He has delivered us from the penalty of sin and given us the benefits of salvation to enjoy forever. For this purpose He was named Jesus, *"for He will save His people from their sins"* (Matthew 1:21).

The Greek word translated Lord is *kurios*. It refers to *the possessor and disposer of a thing; the person to whom a thing belongs; one that has the power to decide for his own*. It also refers to a master. All these describe Jesus, who is not just *a lord* but *The Lord* and Messiah. His obedience unto death earned Him the name (or title) that is above all names, to the extent that all things now answer to Him and are subject to Him (Philippians 2:5-11). The name conferred upon Christ is parallel to the all-inclusive name *Jehovah,* which is translated from Hebrew as *Lord.*

Since Jesus Christ is both Saviour (*soter*) and Lord, it is imperative that those who present Him to men do so adequately. It is not enough to emphasise the benefits of salvation without any mention of the required commitment to Christ's lordship. Truth is, those who encounter Christ the Saviour and recognise the great price of salvation instinctively want to give Him ownership of their lives. This is because one of the main things from which we are saved is *ourselves,* a life governed by self. Until Jesus is Lord over a life, self is very much in control.

Paul surrendered the rule of his life to Christ when he encountered the Lord on the Damascus road. Anyone who genuinely calls on the name of Jesus is expected to do the same.

MY STORY

I remember the morning I gave my life to Christ. The experience was so deep and real. I was not only convicted about my need for salvation, but also about my need for God's authority over my life. Before this time, I was living my own life and making my own decisions; but now the One who created me was staking a claim for the treasured position of Lord and Master over my life.

I am grateful for my own "Damascus Road" experience, the day Jesus became my Saviour *and* my Lord. For more than twenty-five years, I have continued to grow in my knowledge of and submission to Him.

* * * * *

It is not enough to emphasise the benefits of salvation without any mention of the required commitment to Christ's lordship.

I maintain that it is most crucial that we have this fuller understanding of the Person of Christ from the first day of coming to Him. When a believer receives Jesus *first* as Saviour and not yet as Lord (as opposed to receiving Him *both* as Saviour *and* Lord), his Christian walk will always be lopsided. It will take another major episode (and for some, only after much affliction) for such a believer to acknowledge Christ as Lord. This need not be the case.

> "Therefore let all the house of Israel know assuredly that God has made this Jesus, whom you crucified, *both Lord and Christ.*"
>
> **(Acts 2:36 *Emphasis mine*)**

SUMMARY

Jesus our Saviour gives us everything we need for life and godliness;

Jesus our Lord has authority over everything that we have and are;

We cannot embrace one without the other.

PRACTICAL WISDOM

- *How can you be sure that Jesus Christ is not only your Saviour but also your Lord? By acknowledging Him in your daily decision-making.*
- *The essence of prayer is submission to the lordship of Christ, so pray sincerely from your heart: "Lord, not my will but yours be done."*
- *If you are a preacher of the gospel, conduct a review of how you lead people to God. Do not just introduce people to Christ the Saviour; be sure to introduce them to Christ the Lord.*
- *Rededicate yourself to the lordship of Jesus today!*

YOUR STORY

CHAPTER 2

A REVELATION OF PURPOSE

(Acts 9:15,16; 22:12-15)

Following our discussion in the previous chapter about the salvation that is ours in Christ *and* His lordship over us, I want us, in this chapter, to note something else that happened to Saul on the day of his conversion. Remember the question he asked Jesus: *"Lord, what do you want me to do?"* There are others who asked the same question when they had their own encounter with God, but Paul's was a bit different. We will look at two other instances in Scripture.

The first of these two instances refers to those who heard Peter's first public sermon after the outpouring of the Holy Spirit. These ones had asked out of deep conviction, *"Men and brethren, what shall we do?"* (Acts 2:37). Secondly, the Philippian Jailer, after witnessing the mighty acts of God, which He did to set Paul and Silas free, asked the missionary team, *"Sirs, what must I do to be saved?"* (Acts 16:30).

These two enquiries are similar to Paul's, but they are also distinct to some degree. The Jews and the Jailer wanted to know the steps they needed to take towards *salvation* – "what must I do *to be saved*?" The answer they were given also confirms the focus of their question; they were told to repent, believe and be baptised, which are steps toward salvation.

Paul's query, in contrast to these two, was broader. He enquired about salvation of course, but also requested to know what Christ, the Lord, wanted him to do with his life. This is not to say that the others did not receive Jesus as Lord on the day of their conversion; I am sure they did. It is only that Paul's account clearly reveals his recognition of Christ's lordship over his destiny; and having discovered Jesus as Lord, he was ready to take instructions from the Lord's mouth concerning the purpose and direction of his life. Hence the question, "Lord, what do you want *me to do*?"

INSTRUCTED BY THE LORD

The answer Christ gave to Paul also confirms the assertion that Paul was submitting himself to Christ's rule. Jesus had told him, *"Arise and go into the city, and you will be told what you must do"* (Acts 9:6). Evidently, he was told much more than steps to salvation; he was instructed about the direction and course of his life.

As we know, Paul could not just "go into the city" because the glorious light from heaven had blinded his physical eyes; he had to be *led* into the city. He thus began to realise quite early that his life was dependent on God's mercy and leading; not his own ability to chart his own course. He will write much later that *"we walk by faith, not by sight"* (2 Corinthians 5:7).

Those who will fulfil the purpose for which they were created must learn to walk the path that God charts for them and not one that they assume for themselves. It is sometimes easier for us to lean on our own understanding than to entrust ourselves totally to God's wisdom. O that believers will learn early in their walk with God the admonition that says, *"Trust in the Lord with all your heart, and lean not on your own understanding; in all your ways acknowledge Him, and He shall direct your paths"!* (Proverbs 3:5,6).

SAVED FOR A PURPOSE

I need to reiterate that the instruction Jesus gave to Paul on the day of his conversion was more than steps to salvation. It was the command of *the Lord*

Those who will fulfil the purpose for which they were created must learn to walk the path that God charts for them and not one that they assume for themselves.

of his life, and it required his reciprocal obedience. Waiting for him at the end of his obedience was a revelation of the purpose for which God created him. Many years later, Paul would recount this Damascus road experience before King Agrippa, and testify that when Jesus saved him, He also gave him an insight into purpose.

In Paul's words to King Agrippa, the Lord had said,

> "Rise and stand on your feet; for I have appeared to you *for this purpose, to make you a minister and a witness* both the things which you have seen and of the things which I will yet reveal to you. I will deliver you from the Jewish people, as well as from the Gentiles, to whom I now send you."
>
> **(Acts 26:16,17 emphasis mine)**

We can substantiate Paul's testimony from the account of Ananias, the disciple that Jesus sent to him in Damascus. After Ananias prayed for him and baptized him in water, Paul received his sight and was filled with the Holy Spirit – the seal of his salvation. In *addition* to salvation, Paul also received a revelation about his *calling* as a minister. Ananias delivered a prophecy that Jesus gave him for Paul, that Paul was "a chosen vessel" destined to be a preacher of the good news of Christ (see Acts 9:15,16).

Paul testified to this effect before the Jews in Jerusalem. He revealed that the Lord had told him as he lay helpless on the dusty Damascus road, "Arise and go into Damascus, and there you will be told *all things which are appointed for you to do*" (Acts 22:10). He also recounted the prophecy that Ananias spoke over him:

> "The God of our fathers has chosen you that you should know His will, and see the Just One, and hear the voice of His mouth. For you will be His witness to all men of what you have seen and heard."
>
> **(Acts 22:14,15)**

We can safely conclude that Paul was given a revelation about the purpose and direction of his life when he received Jesus as Saviour *and* Lord. This awareness drastically altered the course of his life and became the basis of all his decisions. He embraced this revealed purpose as the reason for his creation – a purpose that had always existed in the mind of God and was now activated by his new life in Christ. Hear his testimony to the saints in Galatia:

> "But when it pleased God, who separated me from my mother's womb and called me through His grace, to reveal His Son in me, that I might preach Him among the Gentiles, I did not immediately confer with flesh and blood."
>
> **(Galatians 1:15,16)**

Paul was separated from his mother's womb but did not understand his purpose in life until Christ was revealed *in* Him. It is the same with every believer today. Our unique reason for being in the world was determined by God before we were born, but only after accepting Christ as *Lord* (not just as *Saviour*) do we begin to discover its full essence.

Paul, I believe, was in a position to receive this divine information because he had fully accepted the rule of Christ over his life. His submission to Christ's lordship paved the way for the revelation of his purpose. If Paul had only received Christ as his Saviour, he would not have received it at that very instance.

MY STORY

As I mentioned in the previous chapter, I had a vivid experience of salvation. Lying on my bed under deep conviction of the Holy Spirit, I submitted my life to God. He knew me more than I knew myself and was able to show me the utter depravity of my life without Him. I surrendered to God and arose from my bed a new person. From that time on, He had the right to direct my life as He willed.

The day after my conversion, I had another unforgettable experience. I began to *write* about the agenda of God for these last days, and how a generation of believers must take up the responsibility of finishing the task of spreading the gospel of the Kingdom. I wrote for *nineteen hours* until I was eventually persuaded to stop. How astounding it was for my parents to see their teenage son do things he had never ventured before! Without any prior love for or skill in writing, I received this divine ability, together with the operation of the Spirit of wisdom and knowledge that gave me what to write.

This experience implanted seeds of purpose within my young heart and birthed in me a desire to pursue the completion of God's Kingdom agenda. Over the years, this sense of calling and purpose, and the essence of the spiritual gifts have become increasingly clearer. I believe the depth to which God's Spirit convicted me, and the extent to which I embraced both His salvation and lordship, paved the way for a revelation of purpose in my heart.

* * * * *

For every person in the Body of Christ, there is a revelation of purpose that God wants to communicate in a direct and personal way. A prerequisite to receiving this knowledge, however, is a *total surrender* to the rule of the Master. God will not waste His words or reveal His pearls of purpose to those who are not ready to appreciate them. The moment any believer embraces the authority of Christ over his or her life, God will begin to make known the unique purpose to which he or she has been called.

SUMMARY

God created each one of us for a unique purpose and the moment we embrace His authority over our lives, He makes this purpose known to us and begins to guide us towards its fulfilment.

PRACTICAL WISDOM

- *The clay does not tell the potter what it is or what it wants to be. The potter is the one who predetermines the use of the vessel he intends to make and goes ahead to mould the clay into it. Stop trying to determine who you are; ask your Maker.*
- *Do not despise the visions, dreams or prophecies that came to you around the time you got saved. Neither should you treat lightly your experiences as a new believer. Can you remember them?*
- *God will usually communicate our purpose in different ways, each revelation confirming the other and building on the previous one. He will always use others, especially those in authority over us, to convey these truths to us.*
- *Every revelation of purpose is like a seed sown in the heart that first takes root and then continues*

to grow until its season of bloom. For this reason, do not be in haste or be anxious about who you are or desire to be. God makes all purposes beautiful in their ordained time.

YOUR STORY

CHAPTER 3

THE PULL OF PURPOSE

(Acts 9:4,5; 26:14)

We have already seen that Paul, from the onset of his conversion, accepted Christ not only as *Saviour,* but also as *Lord.* We have also shown how his total abandonment to God's will opened the door for a revelation about his purpose in life. In this chapter, I want to further underscore the relationship between our submission to Christ's authority *over* our lives and the revelation of His purpose *for* our lives. This interconnection could explain why many believers find the question of their life's purpose rather puzzling for a considerable length of time.

MISPLACED ZEAL

When Paul was busy persecuting the believers in Jerusalem and its environs, he really believed he was doing the will of God. He was zealous for the cause of Judaism and gave himself totally to his convictions about the law. By his own admission, Paul *"advanced in Judaism beyond many of [his] contemporaries in [his] own nation, being more exceedingly zealous for the traditions of [his] fathers"* (Galatians 1:14).

As a Pharisee who studied under Gamaliel, one of the best Judaic teachers in Israel at the time, he was an ardent worshipper of God. "Concerning zeal," he was "persecuting the church" and "concerning the righteousness which is in the law," he was "blameless" (Philippians 3:6). Can you just imagine Paul praying everyday for God to grant him success as he hunted down the followers of the Way!

Jesus Christ was right when He told His disciples that *"the time is coming that whoever kills you will think that he offers God service"* (John 16:2). This was exactly Paul's mindset when he supervised the killing of Stephen (see Acts 7:54-8:1). Thinking God was pleased with his zeal and service, he continued in his rage against the believers and *"persecuted them even to foreign cities"* (Acts 26:11).

The point here is that Paul, before his conversion, really loved God and sincerely thought he has carrying out God's will for his life. He was not a Gentile sinner desperately in need of deliverance from immorality and perversity, but a law-abiding lover of God. Of course, he needed to be saved by grace through faith in Christ; he just did not know this.

Another God-fearing Pharisee by the name of Nicodemus was unaware of the gift or process of salvation until Jesus revealed it to him (see John 3:1-8). There was a tone of astonishment in Jesus' voice when He asked Nicodemus, *"Are you the teacher of Israel and do not know these things?"* (John 3:10). His question to Saul was more striking: *"Saul, Saul, why are you persecuting me?"* (Acts 9:4).

KICKING AGAINST THE GOADS

Before his encounter with Jesus, Paul considered himself a servant of God, but he was actually operating as God's enemy. He thought of himself a knowledgeable man, but knew nothing about spiritual things. He was sincere in his devotion to God, but nonetheless sincerely wrong.

> "Although I was formerly a blasphemer, a persecutor, and an insolent man; but I obtained mercy because I did it ignorantly in unbelief."
>
> **(I Timothy 1:13)**

Another point to note is that Paul had ample opportunities to consider the claims of Christ but chose to resist them all. His learned teacher, Gamaliel, had once warned the Jewish council against resisting the apostles of Christ. His wise counsel could not have been clearer:

> "And now I say to you, keep away from these men and let them alone; for if this plan or this work is of men, it will come to nothing; but if it is of God, you cannot overthrow it – lest you even be found to fight against God."
>
> **(Acts 5:39)**

Paul obviously ignored this warning. Continuing with his self-motivated campaign of hatred, he was among the people that instigated the attack against Stephen. In the course of arraigning Stephen before the high priest and the Jewish court, Paul heard one of the most comprehensive and anointed presentations of the gospel (Acts 7:1-60). However, instead of open up his heart to God, Paul and his horde of persecutors *"stopped their ears, and ran at him with one accord; and they cast him out of the city and stoned him"* (Acts 7:57,58).

Surely, there were many other times when the Spirit of God tried to reach Paul, but he remained elusive until the Damascus road encounter. It is no wonder then, why Jesus said to him, *"I am Jesus, whom you are persecuting. It is hard for you to kick against the goads"* (Acts 9:5). Now this statement is eye-opening. It describes the pull of purpose that Paul had felt many times before this day but had not fully understood.

In other words, Paul was not only following a course that was contrary to God's purpose for his life, he was also rebuffing the promptings of the Spirit that sought to redirect his steps. He was called to be a minister of the gospel and not a destroyer of the Church. He was going to "foreign cities" quite alright, but not to further the Kingdom of God. He was kicking "against the goads" and resisting the tugging of the Spirit due to unbelief.

The Amplified Bible's rendering of Christ's warning helps us understand this point more clearly:

> "And Saul said, Who are You, Lord? And He said, I am Jesus, Whom you are persecuting. It is dangerous *and it will turn out badly for you* to keep kicking against the goad [to offer vain and perilous resistance]."
>
> **(Acts 9:5 AMP *emphasis added*)**

Who knows what could have happened to Paul if he had continued "to offer vain and perilous resistance" to the calling of God upon his life? Things really would have turned out badly just as the Lord warned. Understanding this, Saul surrendered to the lordship of Jesus and expressed his submission by asking, *"Lord, what do you want me to do?"*

There are countless believers in the Church today who are in a similar predicament as Paul was. Things are "turning out badly" in their lives but they do not know why. Could it be the force of pre-ordained purpose pulling on their hearts and affecting their circumstances? Could it be that God had been attempting to realign their lives with His will but they are preoccupied with their own pursuits? This is a serious matter indeed.

THE PERILS OF MISALIGNMENT

Before a person receives Christ into his life as Saviour, and depending on how old he is before seeing the Light, the likelihood is that the focus of his life is already set in a particular direction. This could be a career path, a vocation or a cause to which he is devoted. Chances are that this chosen path is not exactly the calling for which he was created.

For many of us, some of the things that determined our life choices include the need to survive, a desire to succeed, parental influences or a longing to acquire life's comforts. How many have set their hearts on a course just because of the promise of financial gain?

The consequence of these decisions made in ignorance is that at different times, we will feel what I am calling "the pull of purpose." It may be a dream from God, a vision or even an inner sense of dissatisfaction; it may even be unfavourable circumstances that defy explanation. Through these, God will always seek to get our attention, bring us to the place of total submission to His will and align our lives with the original purpose for our creation. When we repeatedly snub the promptings of the Lord, we are like the man kicking against the goad.

The only antidote for the danger of misalignment with God's purpose is total submission to the lordship of Christ. Until we are fully in sync with Him, we will continue to experience the pull of purpose. God, it must be said, does not cause bad things to happen to us; however, living outside His purpose can open the door for the enemy to torment even to the point of death. When we pursue undertakings outside the will of God, we stray from under His covering and become vulnerable to attacks.

Jonah was called to Nineveh, but he went in the opposite direction to Tarshish. Things were turning out very badly for him until he "surrendered" to the will of God and obeyed the instruction to

The only antidote for the danger of misalignment with God's purpose is total submission to the lordship of Christ.

preach in Nineveh. Lot also experienced much hardship as God sought to envision him with a sense of purpose in Sodom. Unfortunately, he did not completely yield himself to God. (I recommend the book, *The Story of Lot,* by Wole Owolabi, because it clearly shows how God gives us many opportunities to submit to His lordship. Jonah eventually got it right, but Lot did not).

At different stages in our walk with God, we will experience this pull towards purpose; the need to surrender more of our lives—indeed, *all* of our lives—to the lordship of Christ. It comes through the tugging of the Holy Spirit and seeks to unleash God's mercy upon our lives. Without this divine intervention, we will continue in our perilous ways and run into untold danger. Severally, Paul acknowledged the mercy of God that rescued him from the consequences of his ignorance.

> "I was formerly a blasphemer, a persecutor, and an insolent man; but I obtained mercy because I did it ignorantly in unbelief... for this reason I obtained mercy."
>
> **(I Timothy 1:13,16)**

MY STORY

Since giving my life to Christ, I have felt the pull of purpose in my heart many times - memorable encounters of grace that increasingly amplified my understanding of God's will for my life and fine-tuned my submission to Him. At times, it was just the gentle voice of the Holy Spirit encouraging me; other times it was the strong hand of God convicting and urging me to surrender my desires and ambitions to Jesus the Lord.

I can never forget an encounter during my campus fellowship retreat (ECU) in 1991. It was my final year in the university, a time when most people think seriously about the direction they want to take after graduation. I had studied Computer Science with Economics and was already considering sitting for professional exams in Accounting. Remember, I loved numbers and was naturally gravitating to this career path.

On this evening at the Retreat, I had gone out to the field to pray after hearing a message. It was there that I felt a strong pull of purpose in my heart.

"Before you got saved, did you have any ambition?" the Lord asked me.

"No Lord," was my honest answer.

"After you got saved, have you really had any ambition?"

"No Lord," I answered again, tears rolling down my face.

"Why is it that now that I want to make use of your life, you have your future all worked out?"

I could only sob uncontrollably.

The Lord went on to tell me that I was not going to work in the field of computing or accounting, that He had other plans for me. I acknowledged His lordship over me and yielded myself to His purpose. Like Saul, I began to ask the question, using the words of one of Watchman Nee's books, *"Lord, what shall this man do?"*

The truth is, I never asked for God's opinion before setting my mind on the prospects of an Accounting profession. This, then, is the point to note: because I never asked God for direction before nurturing a desire for a computing career, the revelation of purpose I once received (the day after my conversion) did not increase in me in the way it should have. There is certainly nothing wrong with a Computer or and Accounting vocation, but it was not what God had planned originally for *my life.* How badly things would have turned out if I resisted this pull and stubbornly held unto my own plans!

* * * * *

DRAWN TO PRAYER

When the pull of purpose weighs heavily upon your heart, it will inevitably drive you to the place of prayer. You will pray earnestly as God's grip of mercy tightens on your soul. At times like this, it is not wise to resist the Spirit of prayer. Ananias was sent to Saul of Tarsus, not just because of his Damascus road encounter or his calling into the ministry, but also because, according to Jesus, "he is praying" (Acts 9:11). The pull of purpose literally releases grace for prayer in the heart of the surrendered saint.

When Saul asked, *"Lord, what do you want me to do?"* the answer he received aligned him with the purpose for which he was created. Years later, He would testify that *"God... separated me from my mother's womb and called me through His grace, to reveal His Son in me, that I might preach Him among the Gentiles"* (Galatians 1:15,16).

When I began to ask, "Lord, what shall this man do?" I was given more understanding about the things God had created me for.

If you, from your heart, make a similar request before the Lord, He will *"show you great and mighty things, which you do not know"* about your life and destiny (Jeremiah 33:3).

SUMMARY

Until we fully submit to the lordship of Christ, the force of our original purpose will continue to pull upon our hearts, seeking to align us perfectly to God's will.

The more we resist the promptings of the Holy Spirit, the more the circumstances around us are likely to "turn out badly."

PRACTICAL WISDOM

- *Do not wait until your life is in jeopardy before you seriously consider surrendering to God's will for your life.*
- *Be honest and sincere when you ask the question, "Lord, what shall this man do?"*
- *Set time aside to pray for the knowledge of God's will for your life. Like Saul, it may help if you add fasting to your prayers as well.*
- *Refrain from blaming God for any negative circumstance you may be facing; instead seek His face for mercy as you yield completely to His purpose for your life.*

YOUR STORY

CHAPTER 4

THE DISCIPLESHIP JOURNEY

(Acts 9:15,16)

The moment Saul recognised Christ as the Lord of his life and the Designer of his destiny, his journey as a disciple began. He did not just become a *convert* to Christianity; he became a *disciple* of Christ. Between the two, there is a big difference.

CONVERTS VS. DISCIPLES

Those who receive Christ only as their Saviour (without a revelation of His lordship) become *converts* and church-goers, but those who receive Him as their Saviour *and* Lord become *disciples* and followers of The Way. After Saul's encounter with Christ, he *"spent some days with the disciples at Damascus"* (Acts 9:19). Afterwards, he moved to Jerusalem where *"he tried to join the disciples; but they were all afraid of him, and did not believe that he was a disciple"* (Acts 9:26). True conversion, one that recognises the authority of Christ over the saint, is the beginning of the discipleship journey. This is the life to which we are called.

Jesus did not send us on a mission to make *converts*. He commissioned us to make *disciples* of people and nations. By disciples, Jesus meant those who commit to learning His way and are ready to do everything that He lived and taught, no matter the consequences or the cost. Becoming like Jesus in all things, which is the ultimate goal of a disciple, has never been without a price – and Jesus has never hidden this from those who desire to follow Him.

Jesus had said to Ananias, the disciple who prayed for and prophesied over Saul, *"I will show him (Saul) how many things he must suffer for My name's sake"* (Acts 9:16). This did not mean, "I will pay him back for all the suffering he inflicted on My Body;" it simply meant if Saul was going to be a follower of *His* way, he had a cross to carry. Jesus did not hide this truth from him, and because he had truly surrendered to Christ's rule over his life, the understanding did not deter him.

"If anyone desires to come after Me," Jesus has clearly said, *"let him deny himself, and take up his*

cross daily, and follow Me" (Luke 9:23). Even more emphatically, He said, *"Whoever does not bear his cross and come after Me cannot be My disciple"* (Luke 14:27). Knowing Jesus only as *Saviour,* the One who delivers us from the burdens of this life, does not mean one has begun to embark on the *discipleship* journey. The journey only begins when we willingly yoke ourselves with Him and choose to learn His ways without any reservation.

> *Jesus did not send us on a mission to make converts. He commissioned us to make disciples of people and nations.*

YOKED TO CHRIST

The true disciple is deeply appreciative of the great yoke of sin from which Christ had delivered him and considers the yoke of discipleship an easier one to bear. An unyoked life does not exist in this world (only in the grave) – we are either yoked to Christ or to the world. In comparison, Christ's yoke is easier.

> "Come to Me, all you who labour and are heavy laden, and I will give you rest. Take My yoke upon you and learn from Me, for I am gently and lowly in heart, and you

> will find rest for your souls. For My yoke is easy and My burden is light."
>
> **(Matthew 11:28-30)**

Saul did "suffer" a lot of affliction as he walked with Christ, but compared to the burden of sin and purposelessness that he had before knowing Christ, it was a *"light affliction, which is but for a moment."* He understood that it was only a part of the journey. In fact, the affliction was *"working for (him) a far more exceeding and eternal weight of glory"* (2 Corinthians 4:17).

There is nothing more glorious than having the life of Christ radiating through us on a daily basis! Hear Paul again: *"For I consider that the sufferings of this present time are not worthy to be compared with the glory which shall be revealed in us"* (Romans 8:18), and "Christ in us" is "the hope of glory" (Colossians 1:27)!

THE MISCONCEPTION OF SUFFERING

Many have come to Christ for salvation but have not yet started their discipleship journey, either because of a misconception about the whole concept of suffering or because they never get told about it in the first place. Having now established that Christ never hides the truth about suffering from those who come to Him, the latter is simply a misrepresentation of His message.

When we entice people to Christ only so they can receive rest and be blessed, and do not tell them the cost of following Him no matter the circumstances, we raise wimpy Christians and not solid disciples fit for the Master's use.

On the other hand, when seekers understand that the lordship of Christ supersedes any worldly allegiance, and takes precedence over the preservation of self, their choice to follow Him (or not) will be genuine. Paul could have decided not to follow Christ when he was hinted of the sufferings that were to follow. But he chose to be a disciple because he had encountered the love and power of the Lord of his life.

In the context of discipleship, suffering is *not* a word to detest; it only implies that the process of change from a life centred on self and its desires, to a life centred on Christ and *His* desires, will, inevitably, be painful to the flesh. When we need to take action and make decisions that God requires of us, ones that are not palatable to the flesh, true discipleship will prioritise the will of God—even if it will lead to some discomfort and inconvenience for a season. The presence of hardship in life does not alter the will of God, neither should it dissuade the follower of Christ.

Another misconception that arises among believers is the attribution of poverty, sickness and the like to suffering. Surely, these are not what

The presence of hardship in life does not alter the will of God, neither should it dissuade the follower of Christ.

Christ had in mind when He made reference to suffering. Are they not the same things His salvation brought for us? Christ cannot deliver us from sickness and poverty only to confine us in them again. This said, even if there are times of physical discomfort or financial insufficiency, the true disciple does not cease following his Lord; instead he appropriates what is already his in Christ and trusts God for miraculous interventions.

Suffering, the type that Paul encountered a lot of times, has more to do with the affliction and persecutions that will come our way *because* we identify with the name of Jesus.

> "Remember the word that I said to you, 'A servant is not greater than his master.' If they persecuted Me, they will also persecute you. If they kept My word, they will keep yours also. But all these things they will do to you for My name's sake, because they do not know Him who sent Me."
>
> **(John 15:20,21)**

THE DISCIPLESHIP CONTEXT

It is worth repeating that the true disciple does not cease following Christ because of hardship neither does he complain because of afflictions in his flesh that are "for a moment." The true disciple allows the Lord to mould him in the midst of his life experiences, for it is in the context of life that true discipleship takes place.

No one manifests patience because of a supernatural gift of patience; the fruit of patience within the believer matures as he daily faces and appropriately responds to situations (and people) that provoke him. Neither can anyone claim to be humble and meek; we learn humility and meekness in the course of our journey. What is the point of singing about Christ's lordship over us if we are not learning to choose His will over ours in the daily decisions that we make?

The priority in discipleship, therefore, is *what we learn* along the way and *our attitude* in the circumstances in which we are learning. The disciple, for instance, learns to *"rejoice always, pray without ceasing, in everything give thanks; for this is the will of God in Christ"* (1 Thessalonians 5:16-18). He maintains an attitude of gratitude in the school of life and ends up becoming more like Jesus, his Master.

What the disciple possesses or does not

> *What the disciple possesses or does not possess, in terms of material goods, has no bearing on his devotion to Christ and attitude to life.*

possess, in terms of material goods, has no bearing on his devotion to Christ and attitude to life. He already has Christ, is in fellowship with God and knows the joy of the Spirit which knows no bounds. Paul said, *"I know how to be abased, and I know how to abound. Everywhere and in all things* ***I have learned*** *both to be full and to be hungry, both to abound and to suffer need.* ***I can do all things*** *through Christ who strengthens me"* (Philippians 4:12,13). What freedom!

The goal of our discipleship is the same: to be like Christ in *all things*. However, the journey will be different for each disciple. We will end up learning the same principles and bearing the same fruit, but our experiences will be unique to each person.

Paul endured a number of years in the "wilderness" learning of Christ. He counted all his worldly advantages as dung just to hold onto the life of faith to which Christ had called him. At no point in his life did he regret the choice he made to follow Christ as a disciple.

MY STORY

My discipleship journey, so far, spanning more than twenty-five years, is very precious to me. I will not trade it for the riches of this world. Its ups and downs, twists and turns, have helped and are still helping me to understand the virtues of God. How else can I understand God's mercy if I had not been needy of it? How could I have known that God is my Provider if I had not needed provision? Can I boast of being patient if my patience had not been tested to the limit? Through it all, my Discipler, the Holy Spirit (and the human vessels He had used), has been a faithful Teacher.

Many years back, He taught me not to waste my prayers on the mundane things of this life. *"Why waste time praying for a new shoe when you can invest it into praying for things that are eternal?"* He had said. Since the Father is already mindful of my needs in this life, I should be free to spend time praying about things that pertained to His Kingdom and agenda on the earth. This lesson alone has made me realise that the life that God is developing *inside* me and the purpose He wants to realise *through* me are more important than the benefits that He gives *to* me. Through it all, I am learning to trust in Jesus and become more like Him.

* * * * *

Knowing Jesus as Saviour is exciting; but knowing Him as Lord is equally exciting! As Saviour, Jesus brings out the sinner and makes him a saint. As Lord, Jesus works on the saint and makes him a disciple.

The true disciple never ceases to follow Christ, which makes him a life-long follower, one who continuously grows and soon becomes a discipler of others, as Paul was of Timothy.

SUMMARY

The discipleship journey does not begin until we are submitted to the lordship of Christ.

The goal of discipleship is that we become increasingly like Christ in all things, and can only be attained when we deny ourselves, pick up our cross and follow Him.

PRACTICAL WISDOM

- *Find out whether you are a mere convert or a true disciple by gauging your attitude to suffering or hardship.*
- *Instead of praying, "Bless me O God," consider praying, 'Lord, who can I be a blessing to?'*
- *Presently, you may not be able to thank God* ***for*** *all the circumstances of your life, but be sure to thank God* ***in*** *all of your circumstances. Later, when lessons have been learnt, you will look back and be grateful for all God brought you through.*
- *Only the discipleship journey leads to the fulfilment of purpose, so decide to stay on your unique path to the very end. Do not be distracted. Do not be diverted. Do not be discouraged. Only be determined!*

- *There is no other way to become like Jesus than the way of discipleship (I recommend you read the book,* ***Becoming Like Jesus****, by Gbile Akanni for more insight into the discipleship process).*

YOUR STORY

CHAPTER 5

THE MISSIONARY MINDSET

(Acts 9:20; 20:22-24)

When a believer knows Jesus as Lord and submits to His rule, a window of revelation opens wide for him, allowing insight about his purpose to flood his heart. Automatically, he begins a tailor-made discipleship journey aimed at transforming him from a *self-ruled* person to a *Christ-ruled* disciple. This discipleship programme ensures that his acknowledgment of Christ's lordship is not just in *words,* but in *deeds* and in *life*. He becomes a living sacrifice totally given to God and His service. Prior earthly ambitions are exchanged for a divine calling to be fruitful in all things unto God and for His Kingdom. He develops the mind of a person on a heavenly mission, one that must count for time and eternity. All this happened to Paul beginning from his Damascus road experience. Evidently, it needs to happen to us today.

THE PREORDAINED MISSION

After three days of praying without any food; after the ministry and prophecies through Ananias, after spending *"some days with the disciples at Damascus,"* Saul immediately *"preached the Christ in the synagogues, that He is the Son of God"* (Acts 9:19,20). He will continue for the rest of his life to preach Christ, particularly, to Gentiles because this was the true reason why he was created. When a man discovers the purpose of his existence, he begins to develop the mind of a missionary – a person sent on a specific, preordained mission.

The purpose of Saul's life, something that his heart was all the while seeking for, existed before he was born. He discovered in Christ that God had separated him from his mother's womb and called him through grace to bear the name of Jesus *"before Gentiles, kings, and the children of Israel"* (Acts 9:15 see also Galatians 1:15,16). This realisation was the basis for the shift in his mind and the ensuing course of his life. He began to understand, and would later testify to others, that he was called *by* God and sent *to* man. In the steps of Jesus Christ, Paul became an example of a missionary who *"was not disobedient to the heavenly vision"* and calling (Acts 26:19).

It bears repeating that when a believer truly makes Christ Lord over his life and truly comes to understand his life's purpose, which is to serve God and be a source of blessing to man, he is inevitably transformed into a person with a heavenly mission. He now has a reason for being in the world. He also has a Lord over him that he wants to please in every way and obey in all things.

> *When a man discovers the purpose of his existence, he begins to develop the mind of a missionary – a person sent on a specific, pre-ordained mission.*

Being a *missionary* for God is not, as some traditionally believe, the lot of a few chosen ones in the church. It is the life calling of everyone saved through Christ. We are all called to glorify God and be a conduit of blessing to man. Wherever we are on the planet and whatever the circumstances surrounding us, we need to live as *missionaries,* people sent on a specific mission. When we live for our own ends, with the bulk of time and resources that we have, it is indicative that the missionary mind is non-existent or not fully developed.

GOD FIRST, SELF LAST

Even in his "spare time," Jesus was focused on only one thing: *"to do the will of Him who sent Me, and to finish His work"* (John 4:34). This is the mindset of a person sent on a heavenly mission. Paul, faced with the prospect of tribulation and hardship, disregarded the risk of personal injury and set his mind on doing God's will. He said boldly, *"none of these things move me, nor do I count my life dear to myself, so that I may finish my race with joy, and the ministry which I received from the Lord Jesus, to testify to the gospel of the grace of God"* (see Acts 20:22-24). This is the mindset of a missionary. God comes *first* in everything; self comes *last*.

Salvation delivers a man from death. The lordship of Christ delivers a man from self-rule. Discipleship further liberates a man from himself and makes him fit for the Master's use. This missionary mindset ensures that purpose is fulfilled daily, God is glorified always and people are impacted in the domain of influence.

One person with a missionary mindset, someone who prioritises God's will over everything else, can transform a generation of people and generations afterward. Such is the testimony of Paul. Jesus had told him emphatically,

> "I have appeared to you for this purpose, to make you a minister and a witness both of the things which you have seen and of the things I will yet reveal to you. I will deliver you from the Jewish people, as well as from the Gentiles, to whom I now

> send you, to open their eyes, in order to turn them from darkness to light, and from the power of Satan to God, that they may receive forgiveness of sins and an inheritance among those who are sanctified by faith in Me."
>
> **(Acts 26:16-18)**

What a sense of responsibility this placed upon Paul! He will later write the following:

> "For 'whoever calls on the name of the Lord shall be saved.' How then shall they call on Him in whom they have not believed? And how shall they believe in Him of whom they have not heard? And how shall they hear without a preacher? And how shall they preach unless they are sent? As it is written: 'How beautiful are the feet of those who preach the gospel of peace, who bring glad tidings of good things!'"
>
> **(Romans 10:13-15)**

The truth is, the destiny of a people hinges on the obedience of a missionary sent from God. People will either go to heaven or hell depending on the faithfulness of those sent with the message of their salvation. Imagine what the fate of the world would have been if Jesus did not obey His Father and lay down His life for humanity? How dark would the Gentile world be if Paul did not

> *People will either go to heaven or hell depending on the faithfulness of those sent with the message of their salvation.*

pursue his missionary calling with diligence? Every person on a mission from God and with a message to man understands the gravity of his God-given mandate. He does not allow mundane cares of this life to distract him from accomplishing his mission. He has the mind of a soldier who wants to please his commanding officer and not the mind of a civilian who wants comfort for his flesh (2 Timothy 2:4).

HEAVEN'S SOLDIER ON EARTH

Come to think about it; a *soldier* is indeed a *missionary,* an officer sent into a region by his home nation to accomplish a specific mission. He does not pursue his own ambitions on the battlefield neither does he opt for the region that has the least level of conflict. He endures "hardship as a good soldier" and lays down his life for his nation's cause.

Our "home nation" is heaven, from where we derive our identity and citizenship (Philippians 3:20). Wherever we are on the Earth is a mission post. We all have specific mandates to carry out under the leadership of our Lord and Master.

Without this kind of mindset, we will find it difficult to handle challenging circumstances and live out our missionary calling.

A missionary, therefore, is not just the believer who goes to a different nation or crosses cultures to win souls for Christ; a missionary is the believer who is far away from his true home (heaven), lives in the world as a sojourner and a pilgrim (1 Peter 2:11), and is consumed with the task of fulfilling the purpose for which he has been sent to the world.

In the life of a mission-minded believer, nothing else takes precedence over the Kingdom of God and its righteousness. He seeks this *first* and lives for it *alone* (Matthew 6:33). He understands that every other concern that he may have is no longer his but that of his sending nation. Paul rightly said that no one *"goes to war at his own expense"* (1 Corinthians 9:7). The welfare of the missionary is the responsibility of the One who has sent him; the success of the mission is the joint -responsibility of the missionary and his Lord. A mission-minded believer bothers himself about the latter and leaves the rest to God.

> "Therefore I say to you, do not worry about your life, what you will eat or what you will drink; nor about your body, what you will put on. Is not life more than food and the body more than clothing?... Do

> not worry, saying, 'What shall we eat?' or 'What shall we drink?' or 'What shall we wear?' For after all these things the Gentiles seek. For your heavenly Father knows that you need all these things."
>
> **(Matthew 6:25,31,32)**

NO TIME FOR WORRY

Worry is an activity of the mind that focuses on earthly things and stems from a civilian mindset. Its antidotes are recognition of the lordship and power of Christ, an embracing of one's assignment from the Lord, and a living faith that the Lord who has called is faithful to provide for every need. Paul, evidently writing from experience, said *"my God shall supply all your need according to His riches in glory by Christ Jesus"* (Philippians 4:19). He did not have time to worry about the mundane things of this life. Instead of worrying, Paul exhorted the believer to *"be anxious for nothing"* (Philippians 4:6).

It really matters the kind of mindset we develop in the course of our discipleship. Those who fail to submit fully to Christ's lordship and their individual discipleship process will not be able to exhibit the correct missionary mindset. When the going gets tough, they will stop pursuing their God-given cause. They will revert back to a civilian lifestyle and become a regular, Sunday-Sunday Christian who only wants to be blessed and has minimal impact in the harvest field of the world. Christ stayed the course. So did Paul. So must we.

MY STORY

I had a life-changing encounter with God's Spirit at the beginning of the year 1991. A few months before then, the Lord had instructed me to organise a conference and outreach programme during the next school holidays, and mobilise students to attend. I had written a short article about *Holiday Outreach '91* (the name we gave to the programme) and distributed it to those I had contact with. Some feedback had just come to me when the Lord spoke to me.

Amongst other things, the Lord said,

> "See how your writing had inspired the hearts of some. *There are yet many who are waiting for you on the other side of your obedience.* Many want to be involved in my work but they need a voice declaring, 'This is what the Lord is saying.' Go, therefore, and be a voice for me."

These words were distinct and powerful; they developed in me a *mindset* that focused on God the Sender and those to whom I am sent. I was resolved that no personal consideration will take precedence over these.

The experience of organising *Holiday Outreach '91* (and *Holiday Outreach '92*), and the insight that came to me in that season birthed the book, *Run Church Run.* They also fortified my conviction that the task of finishing the work of God on earth was the *primary* agenda that the Church has on this side of eternity. All other issues, especially those that concern comfort or status in this life, are either mere additions or subtle distractions.

I am grateful for the grace to discern between God's direction and the devil's distractions. The anchor of this grace is a missionary mindset rooted in the lordship of Christ.

* * * * *

As believers saved by grace, we should have the *mind of Christ* and the *perspective of Paul.* This missionary mindset will ensure that we always say "No" to unfruitful, temporary worries of this life and say "Yes" to purpose-driven, eternal pursuits that spread the knowledge of God abroad. With this mindset in place, there will be little or no conflict with the Holy Spirit who abides in us to glorify Christ and help us fulfil our God-given purpose.

SUMMARY

Submission to the lordship of Christ, a divine revelation of His purpose for our lives, and commitment to the path of discipleship He charts for us are necessary prerequisites to developing a missionary mindset.

Nothing dissuades a believer with a missionary mindset – not "tribulation, or distress, or persecution, or famine, or nakedness, or peril, or sword" (Romans 8:35). Nothing!

A believer sold out to God and His Kingdom understands that his pursuit of purpose will liberate and bless generations of people. This is one of his motivations for obedience and faithfulness.

PRACTICAL WISDOM

- *As a mission-minded believer who understands that pre-eminence belongs to the Lord who does the sending, let your heart declare without any reservation, "Here I am, send me!"*
- *Following the wisdom above, sincerely say to the Lord, "I will go wherever you send me" even before you have an understanding of* ***where*** *He is*

sending you. This is a key that unlocks the door to your Macedonian Call.

- *Develop the spiritual discipline of thanking God* ***in*** *all things, even when you cannot thank Him* ***for*** *all things. This will deal with anxiety and strengthen your trust in God. It will also guard your missionary focus. Usually, you will still to thank God for everything after the uncomfortable season has passed!*
- *Think about the people to whom God is sending you and what the fruit of your obedience could be. How many will come into the Kingdom because of you? What problems of life will get solved because of the grace God has placed within you? Think about these things!*

YOUR STORY

CHAPTER 6

THE LEADING OF THE SPIRIT

(Acts 9:17; 16:6-8)

When Ananias, by the instruction of Christ, prayed for Paul to receive his sight, he did not only prophesy about Paul's calling, he also prayed for Paul to receive the gift of the Holy Spirit. This was an important detail in the assignment that Ananias fulfilled on this glorious day.

> "And Ananias went his way and entered the house; and laying his hands on him he said, 'Brother Saul, the Lord Jesus, who appeared to you on the road as you came, has sent me that you may receive your sight *and be filled with the Holy Spirit.*'"
>
> **(Acts 9:17 *emphasis added*)**

The moment Paul embraced the lordship of Christ, his heart was open for the infilling of the Spirit. In practice, Christ's rule over the believer today is exercised through the Holy Spirit who dwells within. *"No one can say that Jesus is Lord except by the Holy Spirit"* (1 Corinthians 12:3), a confession that must be attested daily by a commitment to following the *leading* of the Spirit. It is not enough for a believer to say "Jesus is *my* Lord;" the true disciple will live out his confession by submitting to the will of the Holy Spirit.

THE COMFORTER

Jesus did not leave His disciples as orphans; He sent a representative to actively take His place in the earth. *The Comforter,* as Jesus called Him, would do exactly what Jesus would have done if He was physically around the disciples. The Holy Spirit will help, strengthen, teach, encourage, intercede for and stand by them. He will be *the Lord* over them. All these He accomplished in the life of Paul who had become a true disciple.

> "However, when He, the Spirit of truth has come, He will guide you into all truth; for He will not speak on His own authority, but whatever He hears He will speak, and He will tell you things to come. He will glorify Me, for He will take of what is Mine and declare it to you. All things that the Father has are Mine. Therefore I said that He will take of Mine and declare it to you.
>
> **(John 16:13-15)**

Through close fellowship with the Holy Spirit, done in the context of prayer and the Scriptures, the disciple gets more acquainted with the will of God; his understanding of God's heart is enlightened; and he finds delight in yielding to the authority of God.

> *It is not enough for a believer to say "Jesus is my Lord"; the true disciple will live out his confession by submitting to the will of the Holy Spirit.*

We cannot fulfil our purpose in life or be a useful vessel in God's hands without receiving instructions from and following the leading of the Holy Spirit. Paul said, *"as many as are led by the Spirit of God, these are sons of God (true disciples)"* (Romans 8:14 *addition mine*).

KNOWING THE COMFORTER'S VOICE

In view of the above, a thorough understanding of how the Holy Spirit leads is crucial for every disciple of Christ. How can we *follow* Him if we do not know *when, how* or *where* He is leading? We follow Him because we are conscious of His leading. Without this awareness, all we will be left with is adherence to a set of lifeless rules. Life in the Kingdom is not about rules, but a close walk with Christ through intimacy with the Holy Spirit.

Jesus established the relationship between following Him (discipleship) and hearing His voice in one of His classic teachings. He said, *"My sheep hear My voice, and I know them, and they follow Me"* (John 10:27). As His disciples (His sheep), we follow Him because we have learnt to distinguish His voice from the voice of strangers. The more we become accustomed to His Word, the more we are able to discern between truth and error; between the Holy Spirit and the legion of strange spirits in the world.

> "The watchman opens the door for (the good shepherd), and the sheep listen to his voice and heed it; and he calls his own sheep by name and brings (leads) them out. When he has brought his own sheep outside, he walks on before them, and the sheep follow him because they know his voice. They will never [on any account] follow a stranger, but will run away from him because they do not know the voice of strangers or recognise their call."
>
> **(John 10:3-5 AMP)**

One of the first steps in correctly discerning the voice of Christ is the *knowledge of Scriptures,* and for this purpose we have received the Holy Spirit, the One who teaches us "all things" (John 14:27). Understanding the Scriptures, therefore, is a major part of discipleship. This is more than the *accumulation* of knowledge; it includes the *application* of God's word to life. Paul placed a high value on reading, studying and applying the word of God. Without these, done through the inspiration of the Holy Spirit, the disciple will not be *"complete, thoroughly equipped for every good work"* (2 Timothy 3:16,17).

In addition to hearing and following God through the Scriptures, the disciple learns to perceive the *quiet witness* that the Holy Spirit bears in the heart of saints. It is no different from the witness that tells us that we belong to God (Romans 8:16). Whether it is the "still small voice" of the heart, inner promptings, intuition or a sense of knowing, the Holy Spirit will always seek to communicate the will of Christ to the disciple. Over time, and particularly through consistent obedience, the believer grows in his understanding of how the Holy Spirit speaks to him. This increases the level of trust the disciple places on this inner activity of the Spirit.

The Holy Spirit also communicates the heart of Christ to the disciple through *dreams, visions, prophecies* and other experiences. He can sometimes speak audibly in the ear, use dark speeches (life parables) or speak through others. He employs a variety of ways and will sufficiently confirm His word so that the disciple will not be in doubt as to what God is saying to him at any moment.

THE HOLY SPIRIT AND PAUL

Evidently, Paul grew in his knowledge of how the Holy Spirit led him. When the Holy Spirit spoke to the leaders at Antioch about his calling as a missionary, he embraced it as a confirmation of what God had previously spoken to him after his conversion.

> "As they ministered to the Lord and fasted, the Holy Spirit said, 'Now separate to Me Barnabas and Saul for the work to which I have called them... So being sent out by the Holy Spirit, they went down to Seleucia, and from there they sailed to Cyprus."
>
> **(Acts 13:2,4)**

Even more crucial was Paul's sensitivity to the Holy Spirit *after* he was sent into the mission field. He always followed the Holy Spirit's guidance. Whatever the Holy Spirit allowed, Paul embraced; whatever the Holy Spirit disallowed, Paul abandoned. This is the lifestyle of a disciple on a Holy Ghost-led mission.

> "Now when they had gone through Phrygia and the region of Galatia, they were forbidden by the Holy Spirit to preach the word in Asia. After they had come to Mysia, they tried to go into Bithynia, but the Spirit did not permit

> them. So passing by Mysia, they came down to Troas. And a vision appeared to Paul in the night. A man of Macedonia stood and pleaded with him, saying, 'Come over to Macedonia and help us.' Now after he had seen the vision, immediately we sought to go to Macedonia, concluding that the Lord had called us to preach the gospel to them."
>
> **(Acts 16:6-10)**

Whatever the Holy Spirit allowed, Paul embraced; whatever the Holy Spirit disallowed, Paul abandoned.

It was not enough for Paul to "go" anywhere he felt was right just because he was already sent; he maintained an openness to the leading of the Holy Spirit and was sensitive to His precise direction. This is why he was fruitful throughout his ministry. When Paul came to Corinth, for instance, *"the Lord spoke to Paul in the night* ***by a vision****, 'Do not be afraid, but speak, and do not keep silent; for I am with you, and no one will attack you to hurt you; for I have many people in this city"* (Acts 18:9,10). Guided by this communication of the Spirit, Paul *"continued there a year and six months, teaching the word of God among them"* (Acts 18:11).

Paul prioritised fellowship with the Holy Spirit because he understood its importance and central role in his life and mission. Out of this fellowship came much insight and experience. It was Paul's prayer for all saints that they equally know the communion of the Spirit all the days of their lives (2 Corinthians 13:14).

THE SPIRIT VS FLESH CONFLICT

The need to follow the leading of God's Spirit creates a line of separation between those who are *mere converts* and those who have become *true disciples*. Because converts have not yet learnt through discipleship to put the desires of the flesh to death, they experience the conflict between the desires of the Spirit and that of the flesh in a greater measure. Surely, both converts and disciples experience this life conflict, but disciples, in the main, because of their submission to Christ and His Spirit, more readily say "Yes" to the Spirit and "No" to the flesh. They have learnt the secret of mortifying their flesh in order to obey Christ (Romans 8:13 KJV).

After Paul's initial "Yes" to the Lord on the Damascus road, he made it a point of duty to do only as the Spirit directed him, even when it was not convenient. One of the reasons why he disciplined his body and brought it under subjection was for the desire of the Spirit to be accomplished through Him. He understood by revelation that yielding to the flesh and disobeying the leading of the Spirit would disqualify him from the prize for accomplishing purpose (1 Corinthians 9:27).

> "I say then: Walk in the Spirit, and you shall not fulfil the lust of the flesh. For the flesh lusts against the Spirit, and the Spirit against the flesh; and these are contrary to one another, so that you do not do the things that you wish. But if you are led by the Spirit, you are not under the law... And those who are Christ's have crucified the flesh with its passions and desires. If we live in the Spirit, let us also walk in the Spirit."
>
> **(Galatians 5:16,17, 24,25)**

> "For those who live according to the flesh set their minds on the things of the flesh, but those who live according to the Spirit, the things of the Spirit... So then, those who are in the flesh cannot please God."
>
> **(Romans 8:5,8)**

FRUIT OF THE SPIRIT

As a disciple consistently obeys God's word and follows the Spirit's leading, one of the results that manifests in his life is a maturing of the fruit of the Spirit, which is the character of Christ. Evidently, we cannot become like Christ apart from the Holy Spirit.

The need to follow the leading of God's Spirit creates a line of separation between those who are mere converts and those who have become true disciples.

As we obey the promptings of the Spirit and apply His teachings to life, His fruit within us grows, the fruit of *"love, joy, peace, longsuffering, kindness, goodness, faithfulness, gentleness, self-control, against which there is no law"* (Galatians 5:22,23). Those who remain babes in Christ do not only yield more to the flesh, but urgently require the life and character of Christ to be fully formed in them (Galatians 4:19).

HOLY SPIRIT EMPOWERMENT

Every disciple learns in practical terms that his God-given purpose and assignment requires the power of God for execution. Natural strength or abilities will never suffice. If we can carry out our vision with our own physical abilities, connections or wisdom, then we do not yet have a vision from God. The things God designed us for are much bigger than us. They require His involvement every step of the way.

What an impossible task the disciples had after the ascension of Christ. As sheep amongst wolves, they were commissioned to testify about the resurrection of Christ before those who crucified

Him. Not only that, they were to convert those who were hostile and make them followers of Christ. As unlearned men and women, they were to teach and disciple those who were already vast in matters concerning the law!

Christ also commissioned His disciples to testify about Him not only in Jerusalem, but also in Judea, Samaria and the uttermost parts of the earth. Add to this the knowledge that the opposition to their mission would be so strong, some of them were going to lose their lives. No wonder Jesus said to them they should not dare to start until they *"are endued with power from on high"* (Luke 24:49). The power He referred to was the presence and empowerment of the Holy Spirit.

> "But you shall receive power when the Holy Spirit has come upon you; and you shall be witnesses to Me in Jerusalem, and in all Judea and Samaria, and to the end of the earth."
>
> **(Acts 1:8)**

Paul's task was also challenging from the start, not just in its scope, but more so, because of his murderous past. He learnt early that he could not depend on his natural talents or credentials. He confessed that *"we are the circumcision who worship God in the Spirit, rejoice in Christ Jesus, and have no confidence in the flesh"* (Philippians 3:3). He totally depended on the exceeding greatness of the Spirit's power that worked mightily in him (see Colossians 1:29).

Paul taught extensively on the gifts of the Holy Spirit, spiritual endowments through which lives are impacted. He said the nine manifestations *"of the Spirit [are] given to each one for the profit of all"* (1 Corinthians 12:7). The Holy Spirit's gifts of inspiration, revelation and power are all needed to carry out our various assignments in the Kingdom (see 1 Corinthians 12:8-11). Everywhere Paul went, he relied on the *"demonstration of the Spirit and of power"* to establish people in the faith (1 Corinthians 2:4).

The sooner we learn that we cannot fulfil purpose without following the leading of the Holy Spirit and depending on His power, the greater our fruitfulness in the call of God.

MY STORY

Early in my walk with God, the Lord took time to teach me how to discern His voice and follow the leading of His Spirit. I learnt about the different categories of "voices" that our spirit is usually exposed to, which are the voice of God's Spirit, the flesh, the world and the devil. I also found a solution to the dilemma we all face at one point or the other: *was that God, me or the devil?*

First of all, I experienced a hunger for the

Word of God and spent much time reading the Bible. This became a foundation for me in discerning the mind of God. (My first published book, *Sharing the Word of God,* highlights the importance of this fundamental need in the life of every believer).

I also found out that the more I emptied myself of this world's affections, the less of its voice I heard. So, not having a longing for a particular brand of car or type of shoe, say, cut out the communications that such longings could send to my heart (that is not to say there is anything wrong with these things). John, in his epistle, communicated this truth with the following words:

> "Do not love the world or the things in the world. If anyone loves the world, the love of the Father is not in him. For all that is in the world—the lust of the flesh, the lust of the eyes, and the pride of life—is not of the Father but is of the world."
>
> **(I John 2:15,16)**

Paul also taught that to accurately discern the good, permissible and perfect will of God, we cannot afford to conform our minds and desires to the world (see Romans 12:2).

Furthermore, I understood from God's word that the devil does not live inside me (if I have not willingly opened the door for him), but seeks to influence me from the outside. There is very little chance, therefore, for any prompting from my inner man to come from him.

The remaining "voices" I had to contend with were the Spirit's voice and that of my flesh. If, like Paul, however, I reckoned myself "crucified with Christ" and committed to dying "daily," the voice of the flesh will dwindle and that of the Spirit will dominate my heart. What then remains is my diligence in the word of God, in giving God inner attention and in my ability to trust His leading from within.

I can testify after twenty-five years that the Lord, by His Spirit, never leads astray. Even when we do not understand *where* He is heading, we can trust in the One *who* is leading.

> 'Tis so sweet to trust in Jesus,
>
> And to take Him at His Word;
>
> Just to rest upon His promise,
>
> And to know, "Thus says the Lord!"
>
> *Jesus, Jesus, how I trust Him!*
>
> *How I've proved Him o'er and o'er*
>
> *Jesus, Jesus, precious Jesus!*
>
> *O for grace to trust Him more!*
>
> - Louisa Stead (1882)

SUMMARY

Without the presence of the Holy Spirit in our lives, we can never fulfil our purpose in God.

The manifestation of the Holy Spirit's leading, revelation and power in our lives grows as we develop intimacy with Him.

PRACTICAL WISDOM

- *Get acquainted with the Word of God; store it up in your heart through diligent, daily reading and meditation. Not only will the Holy Spirit speak to you through the Word, you will also ascertain His leading through it.*
- *Develop intimacy with the Holy Spirit by speaking with Him and listening to Him.*
- *Give the Holy Spirit inner attention. You grieve Him when you continually ignore His promptings in the heart, and quench Him when you consistently disobey His instructions.*
- *Go through the fruit of the Spirit in Galatians 5:22,23. Note the ones that are missing in your life or not abundant in measure. Develop a greater quest for more of the character of Christ in your life.*

- *Depend on the leading and power of the Holy as you minister to others.*

YOUR STORY

CHAPTER 7

THE MACEDONIAN CALL

(Acts 16:6-10)

Developing and maintaining a close walk with God through the Holy Spirit are indispensable in our quest to become more like Christ and fulfil the purpose for which He saved us. If Christ is Lord over our lives, then we need to hearken to His instructions all the time; and to obey His instructions, especially specific direction at specific times, we have to know the voice of the Holy Spirit. Without these in place, the question of fulfilling purpose will be a hit-and-miss affair.

Paul did not make assumptions regarding what God wanted him to do, or where God wanted him to go. He fully submitted to the rule of Christ in his life, was sold out to the cause to which he was called and fully relied on the leading of the Holy Spirit. And because he was sold out to God, he started to obey God's call right from where he was.

GENERAL VS. SPECIFIC WORD

From the moment Paul's life was turned around by the mercy of God, he set out to testify that Jesus was indeed the Christ. He did not waste time at all, but *"immediately preached Christ."* Such was the impact of his encounter with the Lord (Acts 9:20).

The prophecy Paul received on the day of his conversion, that he was a chosen vessel to bear the name of Christ before Gentiles, was a *general* word. It did not tell him when and where to start bearing his testimony. However, the word was enough to spur him into *immediate* action as he began, from Damascus, to share about his encounter with Christ. He did not sit down and wait for a *specific* word about where to begin his ministry and what to say. He began to minister to those around him. He would later testify that,

> "I was not disobedient to the heavenly vision, but declared first to those in Damascus and in Jerusalem, and throughout the region of Judea, and then to the Gentiles, that they should repent, turn to God, and do works befitting repentance."
>
> **(Acts 26:19,20)**

Notice again that Paul began to fulfil his calling from where he was, *among the Jews* in Damascus, before he could engage the Gentiles who were further afield. Here, then, is an important truth about the realisation of purpose that every follower of Christ must be aware of: *until we are faithful in our obedience to God's general call, we may not progress into specific areas of purpose.*

No matter what the *specificities* of our purpose are, we must prove ourselves faithful with its *generalities.* The prophecy God declares over us may speak of great things in the future, but we must first start with little things in the present. There are no short routes to a great purpose that bypass faithfulness in the days of little beginnings.

The Scriptures are full of God's counsel, and every disciple is expected to live by its standards. It may not specify *who* to marry or where to live, but contains everything that pertains to life and godliness. If we are not obeying the word of God and applying the wisdom it contains, it is not likely we will correctly discern direction from the Holy Spirit about who to marry or where to live. In other words, as we treasure and obey the things that God has already *said,* we will be in a position to hear and obey what He is *saying.* Many want to know the details of their specific life purpose but they are not living their lives according to standard of God's revealed purpose.

> *There are no short routes to a great purpose that by-pass faithfulness in the days of little beginnings.*

The Bible teaches many things and Christ has exemplified them with His life. We do not need to ask if it is God's will for us to forgive others; the Bible already says so. Why question whether we need to love our neighbour when the Bible already commands us to do so? It is "all Scripture" that "is given by inspiration of God" and profitable for a fruitful Christian life. Any disciple who desires to fulfil his or her purpose in life will unreservedly and unashamedly commit to observing all the revealed word of God.

Paul was ready to do anything and go anywhere to fulfil his calling as a teacher and preacher of God's Word. He was not trying to impress anyone or show the rest of the apostles that he was also called of God. He simply wanted to obey God by declaring the person of Christ to everyone around him. He was compelled by the love of Christ to speak to men (2 Corinthians 5:14).

From Damascus to wherever the occasion placed a demand on him (which was everywhere!), Paul diligently fulfilled his calling and dutifully obeyed the heavenly vision that he had received. He became all things to all men so that he may by all means save some (see 1 Corinthians 9:19-22). It was in the *general* course of obedience that *specific* instructions came to him from the Holy Spirit.

AVAILABLE FOR SERVICE

After a number of years in Tarsus, his hometown, Paul responded to an invitation from Barnabas and left for Antioch where the gospel was breaking fresh ground. He spent a whole year in this church and, together with other leaders, *"taught a great many people."* The impact of the work was so much that *"the disciples were first called Christians in Antioch"* (Acts 11:26).

When the church needed trusted officials to take relief to the brethren dwelling in Judea, they *"sent it to the elders by the hands of Barnabas and Saul"* (Acts 11:30). Paul proved himself faithful over many years, doing everything that was entrusted to him as unto God. He did not decline what seemed a mundane task just because he had a mandate as an apostle to the nations. Rather, it was while doing the "so called" mundane tasks that his mandate was released.

> "Now in the church that was at Antioch there were certain prophets and teachers: Barnabas, Simon who was called Niger, Lucius of Cyrene, Manaen who had been

> brought up with Herod the tetrarch, and Saul. As they ministered to the Lord and fasted, the Holy Spirit said, 'Now separate to Me Barnabas and Saul for the work to which I have called them."
>
> **(Acts 13:2)**

Paul became aware that he was called of God the day he received Christ as Saviour and Lord, but he was *formally* sent out by God after proving himself faithful over a period of time. Promotion in the Kingdom of God is nothing other than an increase in kingdom responsibility, and Paul always made himself available for tasks that needed to be done.

True disciples do not pick and choose what they do for God or how long they do it for. They possess a servant's heart and relish every opportunity to serve God and man. We are called to service in the kingdom and our faithfulness to this call is what qualifies us for greater levels of service.

The local assembly and the function of its leaders are designed by God, among other purposes, to equip believers for *specific works* of service. A vital part of this equipping process, apart from instruction in the word, is the opportunity to serve in a *variety of capacities*. Those who give themselves unreservedly to *general* service are more likely to discover their *specific* gifts, graces and assignments. God does not use idle souls; He uses those who, like Christ, go about His business (see Luke 2:49). He does not reckon with people just because they have *abilities;* He only recognises those who make themselves *available* for service.

AN OPEN DOOR FOR SERVICE

A God-given mandate is not about titles, but service. It has nothing to do with what people can do for you, but what you are sent to do for the people. Jesus said it best, that *"the Son of Man did not come to be served, but to serve, and to give His life a ransom for many"* (Mark 10:45). The disciple over whom Jesus Christ is Lord will embrace this same mindset about calling, purpose and destiny. He understands that Jesus died for all, *"that those who live should live no longer for themselves, but for Him who died for them and rose again"* (2 Corinthians 10:15).

Paul, as we earlier noted, was already predisposed to doing anything and going anywhere in fulfilment of his calling to the nations. In the course of his second missionary trip, he ventured to preach the word of God in Asia, but the Spirit of Christ forbade him. An attempt to go into Bithynia also met with restraint from the Holy Spirit. It was only after the vision of a specific request for help from Macedonia that Paul had the peace of heart as to where God wanted him to preach the gospel at that specific time (Acts 16:6-10). We may never know why the Holy Spirit closed the doors to these areas, but what matters was that Paul and his team obeyed the One who was leading them.

That a door is open for some work of service does not necessarily mean that God opened the door. Not every closed door is closed by God either. We need to be sensitive as to which opportunities we explore and which ones we ignore. Only the ones that God confirms as His open door, and thus a specific assignment for us to carry out, attracts rewards. How futile it is for one to succeed in something that has no eternal recompense! God will only reward assignments that He assigns.

MACEDONIAN CALLS

Macedonian calls are, therefore, *specific mandates* that relate to a *specific time, place* and *people.* Only those who, like Paul, have proven themselves faithful over time, especially in their discipleship and stewardship, hear the Lord call them to their "Macedonia." And after they hear the call, they are required to be faithful still.

Macedonian calls require the investment of life because the fate of many a people will rest on those who are so called. The called one cannot give a mere portion of himself to his Macedonian call; he must give his all. Only life begets life, and the process requires constant death to self – the giving away of everything. Those who only know Jesus as their Saviour, therefore, are not ready for a Macedonian call. They first need to understand that life in the Kingdom of God is about what we can give and not what we can receive. As Paul revealed, the Way of Christ is that *"it is more blessed to give than to receive"* (Acts 20:35).

That a door is open for some work of service does not necessarily mean that God opened the door. Not every closed door is closed by God either.

Macedonian calls come with the cry of those who are desperate for help. In Paul's vision he heard the plea; *"Come over to Macedonia and help us"* (Acts 16:10). Many need help from the heavy yokes life has placed on them; many need solutions to life-threatening situations; entire communities are desperate for a way out of their multi-dimensional problems. The cries of those slipping into hell fill the spirit realm continually. Oh that many more in the church will hear and hearken to these desperate cries, both from near and distant lands!

MY STORY

In the year 2009, after walking with God for more than two decades and serving His Kingdom in a variety of ways, I heard my own *"Macedonian call."* A door had seemingly opened for me in the United States of America and I was preparing to attend an all-expenses-paid *Writers' Conference.* This was no small door because of the offices of a scribe and publisher that I occupy. I questioned the Lord, "Is it time for the bestsellers you spoke about years ago? Am I going to meet a literary agent?"

The more I queried, the more uneasy I became. I could not understand it. I should be excited about this opportunity, but where was all the excitement? Perhaps it was the jet lag!

In all this, there was one thing I was not prepared to do. I conceded that the Lord must remain in the "driver's seat" of the exploration of this opportunity. The "open door" would not become a reason for me to make assumptions on what He wanted me to do. I would wait on Him and make moves only at His command.

On the third day of praying and battling with this inner disquiet, I heard the Lord speak clearly in my heart. His words were unanticipated and they restored my sense of peace. What the Lord spoke to me became the seeds of my "Macedonian call." The Lord said:

> *"You will go back to Nigeria and start your publishing work there, and be part of development in Africa."*

With this simple instruction, the weight upon my heart lifted and joy filled my soul! Conviction and direction permeated my heart. I recognised the One who knew the paths for my feet. I could now attend the conference with confidence!

Interestingly, through some divine connection during the conference, a "door" opened for me to attend yet another conference three months afterwards – a publishers' conference that had a missionary emphasis. All expenses were once again paid for me to visit Kenya, East Africa, and attend this historic conference – the first time I would visit the region and the first time this global conference will come to the African continent.

Since then, much confirmation and more details have come regarding this mandate. The Lord said we, my family and I, are going back as missionaries; that heaven is our home and wherever He sends us in the earth is our mission field. The work has started in earnest and by God's grace, lives are already being transformed.

* * * * *

Heaven longs to give everyone the opportunity to hear these specific calls to specific assignments, but only the faithful, selfless and prepared in heart will hear and respond accordingly. Many are called indeed, but God's choice is based on His criteria of discipleship and our total submission to His will.

When the earth pleads, "Come over and help us!" and heaven asks, "Whom shall I send, And who will go for Us?" there must be someone set apart unto God that will respond and say, "Here am I! Send me" (Isaiah 6:8). It is only a matter of time before the response of such a heart will become the confirmation that he or she has been chosen by God to make a difference in the region.

Heaven would one day reveal the eternal impact that some have made in their lifetime as they gave themselves to their God-given mandates. Heaven would also not conceal the folly of those who lived for their own benefit and forfeited the opportunity to be a blessing in this life.

SUMMARY

Until we are committed to the general, revealed Word of God, we cannot commit to the specific aspects of our purpose.

Your Macedonian call is a specific mandate, at a specific time, to a specific place, and for the fulfilment of a specific assignment.

PRACTICAL WISDOM

- *Renew your commitment to God's Word – everything that the Bible teaches and Jesus demonstrated with His life.*
- *Do not be an idle believer. Serve God where you are right now! Be active in your local assembly; lead people to Christ; be a blessing to your immediate community.*
- *Is there a door opening for you but you feel the Spirit of God restraining from entering it? Don't force your way through! Wait on God some more.*
- *Understand that you are created for good works and there are a people that are desperate for your help. You will know your Macedonian call when Heaven's beckoning and Earth's pleading converge in your heart. When they do, just say "Yes Lord, send me!"*

YOUR STORY

CHAPTER 8

THE MOBILISATION FACTOR

(Acts 16:10)

When a disciple of Christ that is fully yielded to God's rule receives a "Macedonian call" (specific direction for a specific missionary assignment), the course of his life is altered to fulfil this call. He does not make half-hearted responses or give less than his entire self. Macedonian calls demand total dedication; they require all that we are and all that we have. This is why those associated with the one thus called also get affected one way or the other.

CALLED TOGETHER

Evidently, the companions of Paul embraced the vision that God gave him and considered it their own. They too were prepared to make adjustments in the direction of their lives because of the conviction that God had called *them* together.

> "Now after he (Paul) had seen the vision, immediately we sought to go to Macedonia, concluding that *the Lord had called us to preach* the gospel to them."
>
> **(Acts 16:10)**

God may call one man to carry out an assignment, but in practical terms, it will require more than one man to execute it. Others will need to discover their own God-given task in that one assignment. Everyone will be rewarded equally according to their faithfulness in contributing to the fulfilment of this one call. In other words, it is not enough for the one who received the call to be infused with a passion to run with the call; a whole community of people need to be fully mobilised around the call.

When the Holy Spirit, for instance, instructed the leaders in Antioch to separate Paul and Barnabas for the work to which they were called, the entire church rallied around their mandate and *sent* them into the mission field. They *prayed* for the missionary team and *gave* their substance to support them. They also *welcomed* them back to Antioch and received reports of God's grace on the field (see Acts 15:30-35). The believers in Antioch were full partakers of the missionary mandate of Paul and Barnabas. They became a sending church, a vital organ for extending the Kingdom of God in all the earth.

Paul would later establish the principle that preachers do not go unless they are sent.

> "For 'whoever calls on the name of the Lord shall be saved.' How then shall they call on Him in whom they have not believed? And how shall they believe in Him of whom they have not heard? And how shall they hear without a preacher? And how shall they preach unless they are sent?"
>
> **(Romans 10:14,15)**

CHURCH: A SENDING AGENCY

Whenever God calls a person to go on a mission to "Macedonia," He invariably mobilises others to send him on his way. In fact, as the church in Antioch exemplified, every local assembly ought to be a sending assembly. The role of those who *go* and those who *send* are equally important; both must be taken seriously. The eternal destinies of those ordained to benefit from the call are dependent on the partnership between those who are *sent* and those who *send*.

The Church, as a whole, needs to rediscover her calling as a *sending agency*. We are called to *go* to all the world, which requires a will to *send* disciples to all the world!

Mission agencies, as we know them today, came into existence because the Church aban-

> *God may call one man to carry out an assignment, but in practical terms, it will require more than one man to execute it.*

doned her sending role. In God's original design, local assemblies are the sending agencies because the Holy Spirit, who exercises the lordship of Christ in the church, will always point out those from the assembly who are called for specific assignments. And whenever He identifies those who are ready to be set apart, there should be no hesitation by the church to fulfil her sending function. Paul had his Antioch; every missionary should have his local support base.

I will take this further and say that the sending role of local assemblies is a primary duty. We are not just a pastoral or a healing centre; we are also a sending centre. And because every believer is called of God, we need to equip *all believers* with the mind to ultimately send them out into the world as representatives of God in their assigned fields. These "fields" include cross-cultural fields that are far away from "home" as well as every "field" of human existence in the surrounding vicinity. We need to raise our doctors and send them into the "field" of medicine as missionaries to other doctors. We need to raise our civil workers and send them into the "field" of public service as missionaries to other civil servants. The impact of the glory of Christ will not be felt in society if we are only raising church-goers who do not have a "sent" mentality in the marketplace. Those who have a "sent" mindset will not only see themselves as missionaries, but also be sensitive to the Holy Spirit as He instructs them on how to transform their sphere of influence and introduce men to Christ. (This is a theme to fully explore in other treatises!).

So, the partnership between senders and those who are sent is crucial for the success of every Macedonian call. Everyone who hears the cry from Macedonia must be able to say that "God has called *us* to preach the gospel to them," whether they send or are sent.

SHARING VISION

Ideally, as discussed briefly above, this should happen organically in a local assembly. The one who is called should not be left with the task of mobilising the support that he needs. Of course, he should share his vision and make sure he carries others along with him (which is more or less taken care of if a local assembly understands its role as nurturers and senders in the Kingdom of God).

This notwithstanding, the one who receives a mandate from God, also has the responsibility of sharing the heavenly vision with others so that they too can run with it. Until a vision is shared, it would not come to the awareness of others; and if others are not aware, they cannot participate in the sending or going. In some cases, God will call some to also "go" and be part of the sent team.

In an earlier book, *Run, Church Run (2003)*, I wrote the following:

> When God lays hold on a person, He impresses visions upon the person's heart and entrusts him with the responsibility of running with it. *This responsibility involves the mobilisation of others* whom the Lord has ordained to run together in pursuit of the vision.

One of the reasons why God commands us to "write the vision and make it plain" (Habakkuk 2:2) is to facilitate the mobilisation of others. The clearer a mandate is to the one who received it, the clearer its communication to others. Clarity increases conviction, and a vision shared with conviction enhances mobilisation. Paul was absolutely certain of the commission that God had given him, and his conviction enlisted the support of others. In practice, anyone venturing to obey a *Macedonian call* has to mobilise different groups of people. We will briefly consider some of these vital categories.

MOBILISING FAMILY

Top on the list of those who must be adequately mobilised is the immediate family of the person called to "Macedonia," especially if the call is going to require some form of geographical relocation.

God may call a man, but it is important he gets the support of his family as he pursues the call. Usually, every member of the family, the spouse in particular, will have a crucial part to play, but these roles have to be discovered and embraced. Down the line, all the individual callings and gifting in the family will uniquely combine to fulfil different aspects of this singular purpose. The keywords here are individuality and synergy, without which there will be much friction in the home. What an important issue this is!

Paul, we know, was not married when he met Christ on the road to Damascus, and he remained unmarried for the rest of his life. Free from any domestic entanglement, he was able to remain single-minded in the pursuit of his mandate to the Gentiles. He even counselled others to consider singleness for this purpose.

> "*For I wish that all men were even as I myself...* But I say to the unmarried and to the widows: *It is good for them if they remain even as I am*; but if they cannot exercise self-control, let them marry... *I*

> *want you to be without care.* He who is unmarried cares for the things of the Lord – how he may please the Lord. But he who is married cares about the things of the world – how he may please his wife... The unmarried woman cares about the things of the Lord, that she may be holy both in body and in spirit. But she who is married cares about the things of the world – how she may please her husband. And this I say for your own profit, not that I may put a leash on you, but for what is proper, and *that you may serve the Lord without distraction*."
>
> **(I Corinthians 7:7-9,32-35)**

Is Paul saying that marriage is a detriment to fulfilling purpose and obeying God? No. He simply stated the obvious fact that an unmarried person that is sold-out to God can give *all* his time and attention to pleasing God and obeying his or her calling; and that those who are married *have to* give time and attention to the marriage as well.

Devoting time to the building of ones home is a necessary thing to do; it is *not* a hindrance to obeying God, *especially when, in an ideal case, both husband and wife are sold-out to God.* In this instance, their preoccupation will remain how they can please God and fulfil the divine mandate to which they have been called. *The problem of mobilising the family arises when one of the parties in the marriage is not as sold-out as the other;* or when one is totally submitted to the lordship of Christ and the other is not.

In the case where either husband or wife is an unbeliever and the other is a believer (see Corinthians 7:12-16), Paul counselled that the one who is sold-out to God should not put the other away if he or she wants to remain in the marriage; instead, the believing spouse, through a commitment to love and consecration, can expect the Lord to change the heart of the unbelieving one, and they can eventually serve God together.

In the case where one of the parties in the marriage is totally yielded to the lordship of Christ and the other, though a believer, knows Christ only as Saviour and not yet as Lord, much wisdom is required. The sold-out one may have convictions about a "Macedonian call" while the spouse does not see the reason for such a commitment. The need for mobilising the family is great in these kind of situations. Incidentally, they abound in the church today and are causes of friction in many homes. If not handled with care, they will hinder obedience to God's call.

The solution, of course, is *not* divorce - more so, if the unwilling party is not opting out of the marriage because of the partner's devotion to

God's Kingdom. Paul's counsel to the clear-cut believer-unbeliever case can also help in this convert-disciple case. Through prayer, patience and an abundance of love, the uncommitted can be won over to the Lord's cause. He or she can commence a discipleship programme, learn to prioritise God over everything else in life and join his or her mate in pursuing the call to Kingdom service.

In the extreme case where one party is withstanding the other to the face, the example of how Christ dealt with the root cause that influenced Peter is instructive: *"Get thee behind me satan!"* This should be done in the *secret place* before the Lord and not directly in the spouse's face! And whilst God deals with the unyielding partner, the other's commitment to God need not wane because there is always grace to bear thorns in the flesh for a season (2 Corinthians 12:8,9)!

Even the children in the family need to be mobilised fully. The older they are, the more time we need to spend explaining the Lord's direction with them. We cannot take them for granted and risk losing them along the way to "Macedonia."

Clearly, the mobilisation of family is such a crucial factor in obeying God's call to service. It is always the place to begin after embracing the mandate (unless one is single, of course). As we have seen, Paul had much insight into how the home impacts those who desire to serve God. He wrote emphatically about the characteristics of the man who wants to fulfil his calling, that he should be

> "One who [mobilises] his own house well, having his children in submission with all reverence (for if a man does not know how to [mobilise] his own house, how will he [mobilise] the church of God?)"
>
> **(I Timothy 3:4,5 author's application)**

In other words, the success or failure of a man in carrying his family along as he obeys God's call will affect, to a degree, his ability to serve God to the fullest. It is a reflection of how well he will carry others in the church along with him.

For this reason, every single man and woman in the church should consider their options well before rushing into marriage. It is wise to allow God the honour of pointing out and confirming the right choice. One of the top criteria should be whether Christ is truly *Lord* over the other's life – whether the process of discipleship is complete or has been truncated along the way. The mixture of flesh and Spirit in a marriage only causes heartache and pain. A word is enough for the wise!

The success or failure of a man in carrying his family along as he obeys God's call will affect, to a degree, his ability to serve God to the fullest.

MOBILISING PRAYER SUPPORT

With the immediate family fully on board, the next group to enlist is a team of praying people. (In practice, these mobilisation efforts happen simultaneously and in no strict order). Paul was not only a praying person, he continually requested for prayer support from those who were associated with him.

"Now I beg you, brethren, through the Lord Jesus Christ, and through the love of the Spirit, that you strive together with me in prayers to God for me..."

(Romans 15:30)

"Praying always... for all the saints – and for me, that utterance may be given to me, that I may open my mouth boldly to make known the mystery of the gospel..."

(Ephesians 6:18,19)

"Continue earnestly in prayer... praying also for us, that God would open to us a door for the word, to speak the mystery of Christ, for which I am also in chains..."

(Colossians 4:2,3)

> "Brethren, pray for us."
>
> **(1 Thessalonians 5:25)**
>
> "Finally, brethren, pray for us, that the word of the Lord may run swiftly and be glorified, just as it is with you."
>
> **(2 Thessalonians 3:1)**

The Kingdom of God is advanced on the earth through God-inspired activities that are bathed in prayer. The mobilisation of prayer support will never be too much. Paul called for prayer regularly; so should anyone setting out to affect lives and communities for God.

MOBILISING FINANCIAL SUPPORT

Another aspect of mobilisation necessary for any "Macedonian call" is the enlisting of financial supporters. Again, Paul engaged in this and did not shy away from requesting for support when appropriate. Even though he was conscious of the sensitive nature of money matters and was careful not to bring God's name into disrepute, he still mobilised the churches for the service of giving. He acknowledged those who gave and encouraged others to get involved.

Paul challenged the saints to follow the example of the Macedonian brethren and urged them to abound in the grace of giving (see 2 Corinthians 8:1-7). He even went to the extent of working with his hands so he could make provision for the ministry and set the precedence for a lifestyle of giving among the saints (2 Thessalonians 3:8,9).

MOBILISING WORKERS AND HELPERS

A major necessity for fulfilling God-given mandates is the mobilisation of men and women for the work. As we already discussed, no one has the capacity to carry out a Kingdom mandate all by himself. "Macedonian calls" are too big for one person to fulfil; others will need to get involved in the work.

Paul was always mobilising by the leading of the Spirit. When he met Timothy in Derbe and Lystra, *"Paul wanted to have [Timothy] go on with him"* (see Acts 16:1-3). Timothy ended up becoming a spiritual son to Paul, someone to whom Paul could entrust responsibility in the Kingdom. The story is the same for Titus and countless others.

In his letter to the Church in Rome, Paul had a long list of people to greet and thank, which is a reflection of how he valued networking and partnering with people for the fulfilment of his mandate (see Romans 16:1-24). He recognised every person's contribution and valued their partnership in the gospel.

Mobilising, discipling and working with others are essential parts of any "Macedonian call." How else will the fruit of the work be preserved for future generations? Jesus did not just minister to the crowd; He mobilised disciples, brought some closer to Himself and poured His life into the willing. It was with these that He spent the most time and to whom He entrusted the future of His earthly mission. Those who heard them after His ascension to heaven *"realised that they had been with Jesus"* (Acts 4:13).

Paul told Timothy to do likewise.

> "And the things that you have heard from me among many witnesses, commit these to faithful men who will be able to teach others also."
>
> **(2 Timothy 2:2)**

We have to do likewise.

MY STORY

By God's grace, I am always sharing vision. Whenever I am mandated to carry out a divine assignment, I seek God for the time and manner for sharing it with others. I understand the importance of allowing others to hear from God on how they should get involved.

The big challenge I faced after receiving direction about relocating to Nigeria was how to mobilise my immediate family. Suggesting a move to Nigeria after living in the United Kingdom for close to two decades was not the easiest of ideas to communicate!

However, I have learnt that when mobilising others, we must not interfere with *their* process of receiving assurance from the Lord. We do not coerce or manipulate others into giving, praying or coming along. God must speak to His people. All I need to do is remain persuaded that God had spoken.

And it happened! It was only a matter of time for my wife to receive her own confirmations and grow in her own convictions. The confidence of both of us rubbed off on the children, and now we are fully mobilised to take on our new assignment. All glory to God!

* * * * *

God still has need of men and women today, and those who respond to His call still need to mobilise others for the task. I pray all things be done to the glory of God and for the extension of His rule on earth. Amen.

SUMMARY

A specific mandate may come to one person, but it takes more than one man for it to be fulfilled.

When a vision is plain upon tables, others will have the opportunity to read it and run with it.

PRACTICAL WISDOM

- *Write your vision. Document the things God speaks to you. Conviction grows as you rehearse your vision on paper.*
- *Carry your spouse along as you seek to obey God. If you are having challenges in this area, pray to God for wisdom but also seek godly counsel. Do not break up your family because God has called you to serve Him.*
- *Consider circulating a newsletter among your friends and acquaintances. It is a good way to mobilise prayer and financial support.*
- *Always be ready to pour your life into others. This is the only way you will duplicate yourself and ensure the longevity of the fruit of your work.*

YOUR STORY

CHAPTER 9

A MANDATE FULFILLED!

(Acts 28:30,31; 2 Timothy 4:6-8)

When the Lord gives any of His chosen ones a *specific mandate* to carry out a *specific assignment* (just as He gave Paul a *specific mandate* to bear Christ's name before the Gentiles), there is always an end in view; an outcome that God expects; a result that only His involvement can guarantee. For this purpose, God does not send us out alone; He goes with us. As Paul said, we become *"fellow workmen (joint promoters, labourers together) with and for God"* (1 Corinthians 3:9 AMP).

GOD IS FAITHFUL

Paul understood that his calling was by the grace of God; it was a display of God's divine mercy. He also knew that he could not depend upon his own strength, charisma or know-how. His mission had a risk element from the onset—even a risk to his life—and the Lord did not hide this truth from him (see Acts 9:16). Instead of downplay the dangers ahead, the Lord made a promise to him: *"I will deliver you from the Jewish people, as well as from the Gentiles, to whom I now send you"* (Acts 26:17). This promise proved true barely days into his new life in Christ when, in Damascus, he was delivered from the wrath of those who plotted to kill him (see Acts 9:23-25). From this time onwards, Paul grew in the knowledge and appreciation that, *"He who promised is faithful"* (Hebrews 10:23).

How futile it would have been if Paul attempted to fulfil his God-given mandate in his own strength! It was evident to him from the start, and became increasingly apparent, that *"the flesh profits nothing"* (John 6:63). Paul would say emphatically that he had *"no confidence in the flesh"* (Philippians 3:3). Instead of depending on himself, he disregarded his earthly credentials and put his trust in the power of God. He depended on the *faithfulness* of God and the divine power that manifested through his earthen vessel.

God does not call us to do things that are in our own power to do. He only sends us on assignments that we *cannot* accomplish with our own means. Therefore, every step of the way we would need *His* involvement. Remember Jesus said, *"Without Me you can do nothing"* (John 15:5). As we expect and experience God's interventions in the course of obeying the mandate, we will grow in our conviction, just as Paul did, that God is *faithful*. We would testify like Paul did, that *"He who called you is faithful, who also will do it"* (1 Thessalonians 5:24).

God does not call us to do things that are in our own power to do. He only sends us on assignments that we cannot accomplish with our own means.

That God is faithful means He is *consistently dependable*; it means He is *reliable*; it means He always does what He says. God is *committed* to us and the cause to which He has called us. His faithfulness is the basis of our obedience and expectations. *We believe that God will do what He says He will do* ***because*** *He said He will do it.*

Jesus promised to be with His disciples *"to the end of the age"* (Matthew 28:20) and He fulfilled His promise. He is truly committed to working with those He sends.

> "And they went out and preached everywhere, the Lord working with them and confirming the word through the accompanying signs. Amen."
>
> **(Mark 16:20)**

As Paul's life demonstrated, there are many times in the life of those on a mission for God that the only thing they have to hold unto is a promise from God. What they find in the course of their journey is that His promise is enough, because He is faithful.

Unfortunately, those who draw back from committing to the lordship of Christ, particularly in the face of life's challenges, are yet to comprehend the faithfulness of God in its various dimensions. A major lesson in our discipleship, therefore, one that becomes increasingly crucial in the course of life, is that "God is *forever* faithful."

As we have seen, "God is faithful" means *God will always fulfil His promises.* Paul said, *"For all the promises of God in Him are Yes, and in Him Amen, to the glory of God through us"* (2 Corinthians 1:20). Also, as Paul experienced in Damascus and throughout his life, "God is faithful" means *God will always protect.* Paul testified to his son Timothy to this effect:

> "The Lord stood with me and strengthened me, so that the message might be preached fully through me, and that all the Gentiles might hear. Also I was delivered out of the mouth of the lion."
>
> **(2 Timothy 4:17)**

He also said, *"the Lord is faithful, who will establish you and guard you from the evil one"* (2 Thessalonians 3:3).

For Paul and us, "God is faithful" means *God will always make provision.* Paul said, *"And my God shall supply all your need according to His riches in glory by Christ Jesus"* (Philippians 4:19). He also shared that if God *"did not spare His own Son, but delivered Him up for us all, how shall He not with Him also freely give us all things?"* (Romans 8:32). The simple answer is that *God will always provide!*

Unfortunately, those who draw back from committing to the lordship of Christ, particularly in the face of life's challenges, are yet to comprehend the faithfulness of God in its various dimensions.

Our basic needs for protection and provision are all taken care of by a firm knowledge of God's faithfulness; that He is committed to being with us and performing His promises. We cannot fulfil our mandate from God without this indispensable understanding.

A BASIS FOR COMMITMENT

Until we are *fully persuaded* about God's faithfulness to meet our basic needs, we would not go all out to seek the establishment of His Kingdom in the domain to which He sends us. This is what Jesus taught His disciples when He told them not to worry about this life's needs but to focus on the advancement of God's Kingdom.

> "Do not worry about your life, what you will eat or what you will drink; nor about your body, what you will put on. Is not life more than food and the body more than clothing?... For your heavenly Father knows that you need all these things."
>
> **(Matthew 6:25-32)**

A deep knowledge of God's faithfulness in the heart of a person with a heavenly mandate liberates him or her to seek the fulfilment of the mandate with all diligence. God and His will takes precedence. Everything else become secondary. Such a person seeks *"first the kingdom of God and His righteousness,"* and trusts in God's faithfulness to daily take care of every need.

Paul was totally dedicated to his mandate of reaching the Gentiles. Each time he had the choice of considering his convenience and safety before his commission, he always prioritised the commission. His choice was rooted in the grace and faithfulness of God. Even though he was aware of the constant dangers of "chains and tribulations," Paul could still say that *"none of these things move me; nor do I count my life dear to myself, so that I may finish my race with joy, and the ministry which I have received from the Lord Jesus, to testify to the gospel of the grace of God"* (Acts 20:24). Only this kind of resolve perseveres to the end and accomplishes all that God intends to realise from the call.

> *Until we are fully persuaded about God's faithfulness to meet our basic needs, we would not go all out to seek the establishment of His Kingdom in the domain to which He sends us.*

Paul gave himself to the mandate to which he was called. He sought to save as many as he could, disciple as many as made themselves available, plant as many churches as he could; he did not take the grace of his calling in vain.

Although God is always faithful even when we are faithless, we do not have any excuse for *fruitlessness* in our call. Rather, God's faithfulness should encourage us to do more than we have done before, work harder than we have worked in the past and achieve more than we previously thought possible. This is how Paul lived; he *"laboured more abundantly than"* anyone else (1 Corinthians 15:10). It is no wonder, then, why his life bore much fruit and his fruit has remained for many generations. He was a man who could give this testimony:

> "For I will not dare to speak of any of those things which Christ has not accomplished through me, in word and deed, to make the Gentiles obedient—in mighty signs and wonders, by the power of the Spirit of God, *so that from Jerusalem and round about to Illyricum I have fully preached the gospel of Christ.* And so I have made it my aim to preach the gospel, not where Christ was named, lest I should build on another man's foundation."
>
> **(Romans 15:18-20)**

Before the church in Ephesus, Paul could say, *"I kept back nothing that was helpful, but proclaimed it to you"* (Acts 20:20). Everything he received from God, he gave out for the salvation and edification of others.

What can stop a man with a mandate, someone with the kind of determination and dedication that Paul had? Absolutely nothing! A mere physical inconvenience may discourage those who have not fully made Christ their Lord, but even death itself cannot dissuade the Lord's servant who is determined in heart.

Paul was not for a moment afraid of death. As long as he was in the body, he made his life count for the benefit of others and the glory of God. Paul longed for Christ to be magnified in his body, *"whether by life or by death"* (Philippians 1:20). What a commitment to God!

Nothing could keep Paul from the love of God that saved and commissioned him. He endured all sorts of affliction but kept his eye on the goal of touching lives for God and doing His will.

> "But in all things we commend ourselves as ministers of God: in much patience, in tribulations, in needs, in distresses, in stripes, in imprisonments, in tumults, in labors, in sleeplessness, in fastings; by purity, by knowledge, by longsuffering, by kindness, by the Holy Spirit, by sincere love, by the word of truth, by the power of God, by the armor of righteousness on the right hand and on the left, by honor and dishonor, by evil report and good report; as deceivers, and yet true; as unknown, and yet well known; as dying, and behold we live; as chastened, and yet not killed; as sorrowful, yet always rejoicing; as poor, yet making many rich; as having nothing, and yet possessing all things."
>
> **(2 Corinthians 6:4-10)**

It did not matter the circumstances around him, Paul set his heart on completing his ministerial mandate. And he did.

> "For I am already being poured out as a drink offering, and the time of my departure is at hand. I have fought the

> good fight, I have finished the race, I have kept the faith. Finally, there is laid up for me the crown of righteousness, which the Lord, the righteous Judge, will give to me on that Day, and not to me only but also to all who have loved His appearing."
>
> **(2 Timothy 4:6-8)**

MY STORY

The main theme that God communicated to me during my 19-hour writing encounter was the urgent need to complete the commission Christ gave the Church. In the writings, God expressed His burden for the gospel of the Kingdom to reach the ends of the earth in one generation. He desired to see the kind of disciples who would devote their all to its accomplishment. He longed for believers after the order of *Paul* and *Peter*.

The understanding that came to me was that a few sold-old believers like Paul is sufficient for the completion of the Church's task in a *single generation*. If Paul could accomplish as much as he did with the limited resources that he had, what excuse do we have if we fail to bring transformation to all the nations of the earth with the abundance of resources that we have? How can we justify the meagre results we are having, especially with respect to the quality of fruit we are bearing? (My book, *Run Church Run* largely encapsulates this burden).

Ever since the sowing of this understanding in my heart, it has been my heartfelt desire to be one of the "Pauls" that God is looking for. I want to *finish* the mandate that God has given me, produce an abundance of fruit from the seeds He has placed within me, and contribute to the fulfilment of His purpose on earth.

* * * * *

Paul achieved much in his lifetime, and even when he was confined in a prison, he was still fulfilling his mandate through writing to the churches. He maximised every opportunity he had to introduce people to Christ and establish the saints.

Paul's chains were never an excuse for inactivity or a lack of productivity. He never allowed anything to hinder him from doing more for God. He always put the past behind him and pressed for unrealised aspects of his divine call (Philippians 3:12-14). With this attitude, he was able to finish his mandate and encourage others do the same. *"The crown of righteousness"* now awaits him and those who love Christ's appearing.

Obviously, Paul is justified when he said, *"Wherefore I beseech you, be ye followers of me"* (1 Corinthians 4:16 KJV).

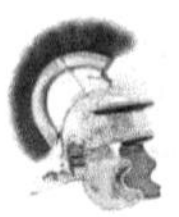

SUMMARY

One indispensable truth that anyone who wants to fulfil his mandate in this life must comprehend is that "God is faithful."

God's faithfulness is the basis for a life unreservedly devoted to His Kingdom cause.

PRACTICAL WISDOM

- *In which areas are you afraid to give God your all? Consider God's faithfulness and learn to trust in Him completely.*
- *Without God you cannot accomplish much. Be sure you are not depending on anyone or anything other than God and His faithfulness.*
- *What opportunities do you presently have to do more for God? Make the most of them as they do not remain forever.*
- *Do you want to be one of the "Pauls" that God is looking for in these last days? Find that one thing He has created you to do, and do it with all your life. Discover your "Macedonia" and empty your life for His glory.*

YOUR STORY

Did you enjoy and gain wisdom from reading

THE MANDATE OF PAUL?

Do you want to write the author

and share your story?

Please write to the following email address:

publishwithsophos@gmail.com

MORE TITLES FROM SOPHOS BOOKS

By Tokunbo Emmanuel

- The Secret of Abraham

- The Wells of Isaac

- The Destiny of Jacob

- The Mandate of Paul

By Wole Owolabi

- The Story of Lot

For enquiries or comments:

publishwithsophos@gmail.com

Raising the voice of Wisdom
to all mankind.

www.ingramcontent.com/pod-product-compliance
Lightning Source LLC
LaVergne TN
LVHW010104110826
845155LV00028B/469
* 9 7 8 1 9 0 5 6 6 9 2 1 9 *